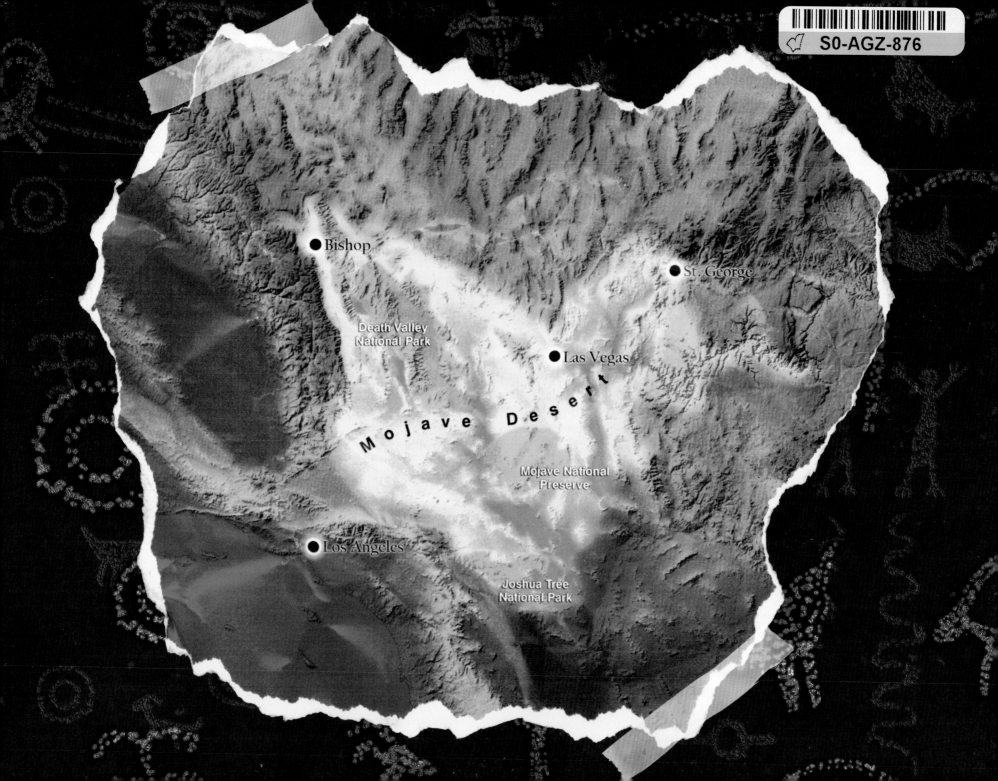

Desert Seasons

A Year in the Mojave

Journaled and Sketched by Ruth K. A. Devlin
Nature Photography by Frank Serafini
A Las Vegas Review-Journal Book

A Las Vegas Review-Journal Book

Cataloging-in-Publication Data Available

For Tina —
The beauty of the
Mojave awaits you —
Enjoy!
Ruth Devlin
'03

Edited by Tina Littell and A. D. Hopkins

Book Design by Evan Fields
Printed in Hong Kong

Stephens
Press LLC

A Stephens Media Group Company • Post Office Box 1600 • Las Vegas, Nevada 89125-1600

Desert Seasons

A Year in the Mojave

Ruth's Dedication: For my children, Nathan and Katie — my hiking partners forever!

Frank's Dedication: To my friend and mentor, Robert Lievens, who helped me learn how to see.

Introduction

There are four major deserts in North America — the Great Basin, the Mojave, the Sonoran and the Chihuahuan. These deserts inhabit the southwestern United States and extend into Mexico. Cities have sprung up along their edges, and sometimes in their middles. Not every desert is covered with sand dunes, and the seasons in the deserts of North America are unlike those in other biomes. Deep snow-covered earth is not the signal of winter. When you live in the desert, large trees with changing red, burnt orange and yellow leaves are not the signs of fall. Summer does not always bring intense greenery, and the soft showers of spring are not the norm.

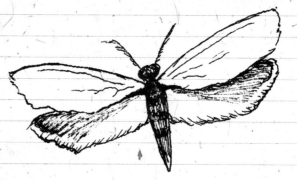

I moved to the Mojave 24 years ago, having grown up with the four distinct seasons of Indiana. I watched the Midwestern seasons change with great fanfare, and when I first moved to the desert, I missed those grand seasonal changes. What I first saw was an unchanging brown landscape with only cold days and hot days to mark the passing months. Over the years I discovered that here in the Mojave there are seasonal changes, but because they do not trumpet their arrival, I must be quiet and watch carefully to see when Mother Nature changes her cloaks.

The physical area of the Mojave is only approximately 35,000 square miles — the size of Maine, or (interestingly enough, given my roots) Indiana, but the Mojave holds a vast array of plant species. Almost one-quarter of the plants found within the Mojave are endemic — which means that they grow nowhere else, and there are about one hundred rare species of plants. It is easy to think of the typical desert floor plants (cactus, shrubs, desert wildflowers), but at higher elevations the Mojave holds juniper trees and piñon pines.

The Mojave Desert is a wondrous and exciting place. It is fragile and tenacious. It is a desert to be wondered at and hiked and drawn and photographed. I hope that you will enjoy seeing it as I do, through the words and drawings from my journals, and the photographs of my friend Frank as we journey through a year in the Mojave.

— Ruth K. A. Devlin

Introduction

Photographing the desert landscape presents the visual artist with unique challenges. Dramatic temperatures, ranging from near zero in the winter months to over one hundred degrees in the summer, can wreak havoc on one's equipment and one's body. Due to the fact that deserts receive less than ten inches of rain a year, finding dramatic clouds to enhance desert images is a challenge. However, at dawn and dusk, when the sun's rays are golden and the light is soft, the red rocks glow, the cactus look greener and the sky can dance with magic colors. It is for these reasons that I choose to walk among the creosote and Joshua trees, to wander down lonely arroyos and narrow canyons, in order to bring to life the desert in my images.

Frank Serafini

December 5th

It's raining, and everyone is thrilled. Rain is a very big deal in the desert. I remember living in Indiana, and when it rained there, no one got excited — in fact, they tended to be quite gloomy about it.

Winter rain is especially important for the desert because of what it means for the coming spring. Seeds know how to sit, waiting underground, in cracks, and in other small hiding places; waiting to soak up the winter rains that will give them permission to germinate, and the ability to bloom in the spring. Some seeds can sit for years. The cacti will also hang on tenaciously to any water that they receive in the winter — using it to feed themselves during times of little moisture.

Come next spring, if we get enough rain this winter, there will be flowers; flowers of every shade and hue imaginable; flowers of such intense color that they will take your breath away.

December 18th

In the broad sweeping expanses of the Mojave I can
see the dusk being gathered — the gathering dusk.
The daylight moves across the flat expanses — the
basins that lie between the mountain ranges — moving
from bright light to soft golden hues.
As the light glides across the valley floor, it
plays a quick game of hide and seek with the
desert plants, who will hold its warm hand
for one last moment before the day finally
rests on the western mountain — dimming
down to night.

Who is the gatherer?

January 7th

I love the early morning minutes that slide between dawn's darkness and morning's full glory. As the sun rises up to greet the day the desert has a chance to flaunt her beauty — bathing the desert scrub and rocky floor with soft, gentle tones of pink and salmon.

There's no sign of the sun in the east as I sit and write under the slowly brightening sky, and the mountains in the west are glowing with the deep gold of a ripe peach. Their peaks are brilliant — on fire with the sun's light — but where is the sun itself? I glance to the east and although the sun's light has touched the sky, there is no radiant ball to be seen. How can the western mountains be lit if the sun is still behind the mountains that lie to the east? Here then is another secret the desert holds about herself.

January 23rd

Desert Winter Haiku

All morning the clouds

Have hung and now they lift to

Show their gift of snow

February 15th

Sometimes
the sun hits the Red Rocks just so —
Like on a stormy February day —
and the snow-filled clouds
lie heavy between the craggy peaks.
while sunbeams, breaking away from their
    cloudy confines,
slice between the ridges
making each peak look like a construction
    paper cutout.

February 26th

Winter
brings clouds
seldom seen in summer.
Today flat-bottom clouds float
above the mountain tops. Only the highest peaks
can reach up to poke their noses into the soft, puffy grayness.

Desert Facts

- A desert can in part be defined as being a place that gets less than ten inches of precipitation a year.
- The Mojave gets only one to five inches of rain per year.
  — Most of the year's rain falls in winter.
  — One area in the Mojave got no rain for over two years — from October 3, 1912 until November 8, 1914.
- The Mojave is called a rain shadow desert because the desert sits in the "shadow" of the western mountains, which stop the rain and make it a desert.
  — A rain shadow desert is created when there are mountain ranges that lie parallel to the coastal areas. The winds cool as they rise up the mountains, and clouds are formed. The moisture falls on the mountainsides facing the coast, and when the air finally makes it over to the other side of the mountain it is quite dry.

March 3rd

It isn't that the desert has no spring
but rather
she holds it close to her heart —
protecting it,
tending it like a mother
with her young child.

Sometimes, if you look on just the
right day
and in just the right spot,
you can see the desert trees bud —
a tight tiny birth
from which small desert leaves will blossom.

And if the winter rains have been perfect,
and the fall temperatures have been
exactly right,
the cactus flowers will show themselves;
and like a child's first piano recital
the music is short-lived —
but filled with glory.

It isn't that the desert has no spring,
but rather
you just need to know
How to feel it ...
When to see it ...
And where to look.

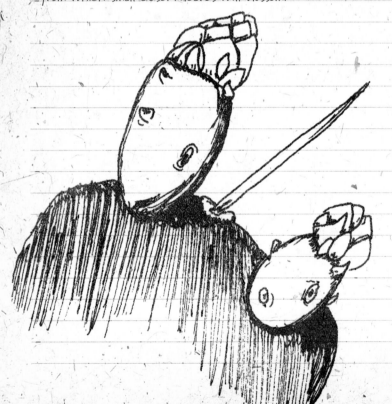

March 17th

The desert flowers have begun their show.
It's seasonal,
      and tickets are hard to come by because the start date is so uncertain,
         and the location is always a bit off the beaten path.
They won't all show themselves on the same day,
      but quietly they will unfurl when they think the time is right —
         some for only a few hours.
From amid the thorns will come petals of deep scarlet, and orange, soft yellow, and magenta.
Slender ocotillo branches will present delicate red bells —
      shooting out to an explosion of yellow.
There will be clusters of purple feather dusters and
Tiny pink blossoms masquerading as young ladies' ball gowns,
And glowing golden poppies, consistently perfect in their graceful carriage.
The flowers are the stars of the show —
      the heralds of spring —
         and we welcome them
            on whatever day they
               decide to come.

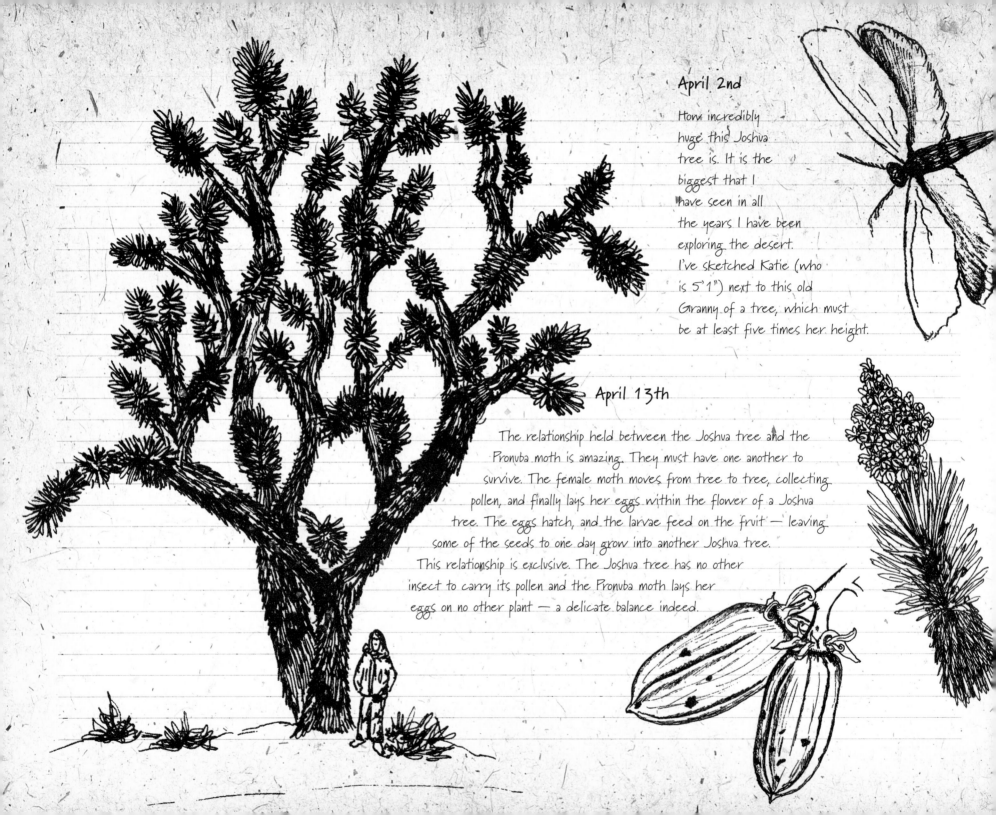

April 2nd

How incredibly huge this Joshua tree is. It is the biggest that I have seen in all the years I have been exploring the desert. I've sketched Katie (who is 5'1") next to this old Granny of a tree, which must be at least five times her height.

April 13th

The relationship held between the Joshua tree and the Pronuba moth is amazing. They must have one another to survive. The female moth moves from tree to tree, collecting pollen, and finally lays her eggs within the flower of a Joshua tree. The eggs hatch, and the larvae feed on the fruit — leaving some of the seeds to one day grow into another Joshua tree. This relationship is exclusive. The Joshua tree has no other insect to carry its pollen and the Pronuba moth lays her eggs on no other plant — a delicate balance indeed.

Joshua Tree Facts

- They grow best on flat or gently sloping terrain between 2,000 and 4,000 feet.
- Joshua trees can be 32 feet high with trunk circumference of 12 feet.
- There are no growth rings so it's hard to tell the age — but experts think that one in Joshua Tree National Park may be 900 years old.
- The shallow root system and top heavy branches make them unsteady.
- With appropriate temperature and moisture they can bloom from late February to early May.
- The waxy, creamy-colored, bell-shaped flowers are approximately 1.5 inches with three sepals, and three petals, crowded together on many branched clusters.
- The 2.5-4 inch, three-celled fruit is light greenish and holds flat, black seeds which dry and fall in late spring.
- Most Joshua trees begin their life under the protection of a bush.
- Pioneers thought the plant suggested the Prophet Joshua raising his arms toward the Promised Land.

May 8th

On this warm sunny May day we are in search of a waterfall, and after spending the night in Panamint Springs in Death Valley National Park, we start our hike to Darwin Falls. With our knapsacks filled with lunches and plenty of water we start down a dry, wide, gravelly canyon. It's criss-crossed with deep ravines telling us that rushing flood water has made its way through here, although I sense from the dryness of the sand that it was quite some time ago.

The sides of the canyon are dotted with agaves and families of barrel cactus. Soon we find ourselves maneuvering through tall reeds and grasses which tell us that there is water underground that must be close to the surface. I think we are almost to our destination! The reeds grow close together, and along with the invisible scurrying desert creatures that we can hear, we are hidden from view as we hike up the narrowing canyon.

We begin to see the water in a narrow stream on the surface, with white and yellow wildflowers filling its edges. Just as we start to think that the trail is too narrow and rocky for us to explore farther, the way opens up and we come upon a cool deep blue pool. The waterfall rushes down — a white veil over ancient stone and green moss — before it splits into two and feeds the pool. It seems a miracle to find this here! The tall trees and the towering walls above offer us a deep shade. The air is cool and the quiet invites us to sit and reflect as the frogs croak us a water song. Ahh. Water in the desert.

Cactus Facts

- Barrel cacti germinate only when the weather conditions are precisely correct. This means that the barrel cacti near each other are all approximately the same age.
- Desert animals use the cactus pads as a source of moisture — they can bite through the waxy outer covering to the juicy inside flesh.
- People eat cactus too. The pads of prickly pear cactus are quite tasty; they're called nopalitos.
  - First the thorns must be cut out (a very time-consuming task), and then the pads are cooked.

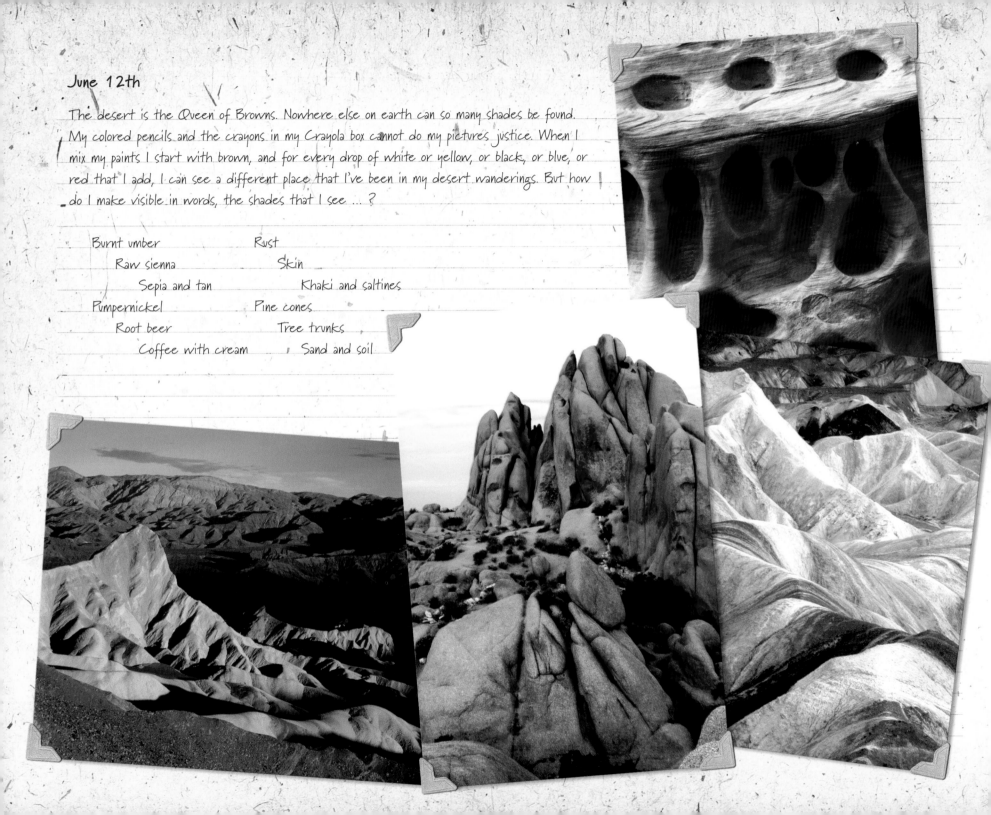

June 12th

The desert is the Queen of Browns. Nowhere else on earth can so many shades be found. My colored pencils and the crayons in my Crayola box cannot do my pictures justice. When I mix my paints I start with brown, and for every drop of white or yellow, or black, or blue, or red that I add, I can see a different place that I've been in my desert wanderings. But how do I make visible in words, the shades that I see ... ?

Burnt umber	Rust
Raw sienna	Skin
Sepia and tan	Khaki and saltines
Pumpernickel	Pine cones
Root beer	Tree trunks
Coffee with cream	Sand and soil

June 24th

Today I saw four quail!
Not one or two,
but four Gambel's quail
scurrying across the road.

For me this was a first,
and Byrd Baylor would say
that it should be a celebration,
and I agree!

So I dub today,
June 24th,
as
"Quail Day."

Their curved head feathers
bent forward in a
prim and fashionable way
and they wiggled slightly as they scampered.

It seemed impossible,
that they should have
such fast little legs,
that all moved in tandem;

And they reminded me of
four little old ladies on their way to tea
with their best new bonnets on —
but unfortunately, they all bought the same hat.

June 28th

The creosote is an unassuming plant with a tenacity that is admirable. It is the creosote that sends its pungent fragrance out to scent the desert after a rain. Some days, when the warm rain has fallen only in the upper elevations, the desert winds float the creosote smell down to the dry valleys. We here in the desert call it "the smell of rain." It is a deep smell that awakens the senses, and conjures up visions of drenching rainfalls that saturate a body's need for moisture. It is a scent that I have found nowhere else in the world, and it, above all other smells, tells me that I am in the desert.

Creosote Facts

- The creosote covers three-quarters of the Mojave (which includes all of the lower elevation areas).
- It cannot tolerate extreme cold, and it could be better than the Joshua tree at showing us where the Mojave's northern boundary joins with the Great Basin Desert.
- The creosote withstands extreme heat and drought perhaps better than most other desert plants.
  — When drought occurs, the leaves of the creosote fold in half to guard against moisture loss, and during times of extended drought, the leaves fall off completely.
- Creosote bushes spread themselves out with perfect symmetry in "fairy rings" across the desert floor — the mother plant sends out roots that clone into other creosote bushes that form a ring around the mother plant.
  — King Clone's ring is 75 feet across.
  — Although it is difficult to be sure, it is possible that some clones in the Mojave date back 9,000 years.
- The root systems are wide — they can extend 50 feet.
- Animals will burrow under the bush, and jackrabbits will eat the branches — but not the leaves.

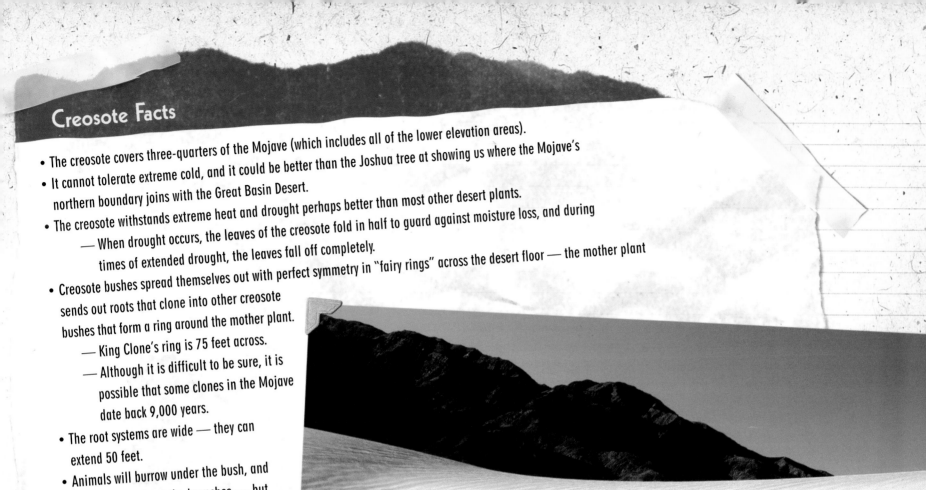

July 13th

The summer allows us to watch giant cumulus clouds form over the mountains. Because of the dry desert air that rises, it is not often that they are able to actually deposit their moisture on the desert floor. Some days we can see the rain sheets falling from the clouds — drying out before they can find the earth. When the clouds do decide to dump rain in the mountains, flash flooding can occur, moving giant boulders, uprooting trees, and changing the face of the Mojave basins. When we're lucky, the summer rains make it all the way to the valleys, and then leave us a rainbow — the ribbon on a desert gift.

July 22nd

The white puffy clouds have been replaced.
They looked so friendly —
Like swimming turtles, and smiling old men,
and apple trees laden with fruit.
They've been replaced by flat-bottom
Black indigo clouds —
the kind that cover the sky,
and shoot lightning down to the desert floor —
The kind that actually
Might
Hold
Rain.

Desert Plant Facts

Desert plants have many ways to stay alive during the hot summer months — periods of time without rain, and of scorching temperatures.

- Cacti store moisture that they have received during periods of rain and use it during the months of little rain.

- Survival tactics can cost a cactus growth — at times it may grow only one-quarter inch per year.

- Cacti and other desert shrubs can either have a shallow root system to get any rainfall that filters down through the tough desert soil, or a long taproot to find moisture deep within the earth.
    — The waxy coating on some cacti helps them to resist evaporation, and the sunken pores close during the hot days and open at night.
    — Some cacti have spines closely spaced to help shade the plant from the hot desert sun.

- Desert plants often have smaller leaves — this provides less surface for the sun to burn and dehydrate the plant.

August 10th

I'm sure I shouldn't complain.
I know I'm lucky to live
where the air is dry,
and the wide open spaces
lift up their voices
to call me out to see.
I know I'm blessed
to live where I can actually see
the geology of the land
exposed to the sky.
I know I'm one of the few
who will ever get to see
the desert's gift of flowers in
   the spring,
or smell the creosote's message
of coming rain across the
   desert floor.

I'm sure I shouldn't complain., but it's
Just
So
Hot.
And I'm tired of it being hot.
I know there are people who live
   where the sun seldom shines,
and it rains all the time,
who would love to have some of this
Dry
White
Heat.
And since I'm quite done being hot
I think
I'm willing
to share!

September 18th

The summer is fading
like an old denim shirt.
The days are not so glaringly, blindingly, searingly hot.
Instead, the sharp edges of the light are tempered by the coming of fall,
which is quietly making an entrance.
This morning when I woke
it was only 82 degrees,
and a light breeze made the leaves shiver.
Funny to shiver when it's 82 degrees.

Lizard Heaven:
The lizards belong here.
They love the sun
and the open spaces.
They wear camouflage skins of understated elegance —
Zebra tails,
  collared necks,
        and blue underbellies that mirror the desert sky.
I think that
to bask on a rock
in the warm September sun
without fear of a hawk or a roadrunner near
would most certainly be heaven
for a lizard.

October 19th

Death Valley is full of visual surprises! We're on our way home after a weekend adventure, and as we drive along the road that runs through the park, the rocky desert floor suddenly presents sand dunes that swirl away from us toward the mountains in the north. I stop the car and we get out to hike — everyone knows that to experience the desert you must not simply view it from the window of a car.

The Mojave is not characterized by endless expanses of sand dunes like the Sahara or the Gobi, and so although they seem out of place here it is easy to connect Death Valley's dunes with the notion of desert. They are startlingly beautiful! Their bleached whiteness and eddying wind curves are complemented by the intense blue of the desert's autumn sky. It's mind-boggling to think that each tiny grain represents a piece of geologic history — reduced from larger rocks over time by weather and moved by wind across the desert floor to this point.

October 29th

Tortoise.
Elusive tortoise with patterned shell,
You are a gentle desert dweller,
  A cactus nibbler,
    flower eater,
      and wilderness explorer.
As the fall begins its journey into the Mojave
You entertain thoughts of hibernating —
Sleeping until spring
In your deep, dark burrow.
I wonder
While you sleep beneath the ground —
Of what do you dream?

November 6th

The distant hills are
Gently folded like
A wool sweater,
Nubby with sage and creosote
Honey colored in
The afternoon light.

November 22nd

The sun goes down to bed.
What meager heat it shared with the day
goes with it to blanket the stars —
The children of the sun.

Ruth K. A. Devlin

Ruth Devlin lives in Las Vegas, Nevada with her husband and two children. She is a Southern Nevada Writing Project fellow and full-time primary English Language Learner (ELL) teacher. When she's not teaching or involved with family activities she enjoys writing, drawing, reading, carving, and hiking.

Frank Serafini

Dr. Frank Serafini is an Assistant Professor of Literacy Education and Children's Literature at the University of Nevada-Las Vegas. He spends his free time playing his guitar, reading everything and traveling to his favorite locations to create new landscape images.